Perseverance and God's Faithfulness

Read Jan 2019

This booklet is taken from the last known sermon preached
by Jamie Buckingham in January 1992,
about a month before his death.

You can listen to this message and others at:
www.jamiebuckinghamministries.com

Perseverance and God's Faithfulness

by

Jamie Buckingham

Risky Living Ministries, Inc.

Perseverance and God's Faithfulness
By Jamie Buckingham
Edited for print by Bruce Buckingham

Copyright © 2017 by Risky Living Ministries, Inc.

Unless otherwise noted, scripture quotes are taken from THE HOLY BIBLE, NEW INTERNATIONAL VERSION®, NIV® Copyright © 1973, 1978, by Biblica, Inc.® Used by permission. All rights reserved worldwide.

Published by Risky Living Ministries, Inc.
3901 Hield Road NW
Palm Bay, FL 32907

www.RiskyLivingMinistries.com

Risky Living Ministries is dedicated to preserving the teachings and life works of Jamie Buckingham.

Cover photo by Bruce Buckingham

ISBN-10: 1546950435

Perseverance
and God's Faithfulness

Thank you for your prayers. I have needed them to fulfill my promise to you that I would report back to you on the physical progress I am making.

Once again, I've spent this last week in St. Petersburg, Florida, with my friend Dr. Ralph Johnson, who is a radiologist. Dr. Johnson has been administering the radiation to my liver to combat the cancer that doctors found there. I also received another dose of chemotherapy.

Earlier this week the doctors did another blood test to determine if there is abnormal activity in my liver, and if so, how much abnormal activity there is. For a healthy man, the normal range for that test is up to 140-something. That's the number to not exceed in the normal range. A couple of weeks ago, my number was as high as 470. It was out of range for a normal count but "not alarming," the doctor said. "It could go much higher than that," he said, trying to reassure me.

This last week, after two weeks of treatment, they gave me another test, and the number had dropped 20 percent, down to 370. The doctors said they could in no way give credit to the medical treatment, because I'd not been receiving treatments long enough. "There must be another force at work," one doctor said. So, I give thanks and praise God for that report.

In the meantime, my body is reacting strangely to all the medications they are giving me. I get terribly weary. I've never been tired like this before. I've gotten sleepy, but I've never gotten truly physically tired—certainly not like this.

I'm at the point — as I have always tried to be — of trusting God through it all.

At about 4 o'clock in the afternoons, I get tired. By 7 o'clock I want to go to bed, which is what I did yesterday. The further away I get from the treatments, however, the better I feel. I'm feeling much better today.

The doctors also said that my white blood count is down, and I need to stay away from people who have infectious diseases since I'm very susceptible to them. So, you will have to excuse me if I stand off a little when we speak.

But all in all, it's been a good week. I go back this coming week for additional treatments, and then I'll probably have another CT scan. They want to see exactly what's going on with the cancer in my liver. So, we're going to wait and see. I'm at the point—as I have always tried to be—of trusting God through it all.

In the meantime, I've developed a dryness in my throat, which means I cough a lot. So, if I cough into the microphone, please forgive me this morning. I'm sucking on all kinds of little cough lozenges to prevent that from happening.

Now, I want you to stand and repeat after me:

"The mission of this church is to love God. Enjoy Him forever. Hear what He is saying and do what He is doing."

Repeat it once more:

"The mission of this church is to love God. Enjoy Him forever. Hear what He is saying and do what He is doing."

Thank you. You may be seated.

Love God, Enjoy Him forever.
Hear what He is saying and
do what He is doing.

Jackie and I were sitting in our den last night. We were supposed to go to three weddings yesterday afternoon and didn't get to any of them. I just determined that I wasn't going to push myself beyond my limits of endurance. We were also supposed to come up here last night for a wonderful birthday party for one of our staff members who just turned 50. I won't tell you who she is, but she's sitting right back there and has blonde hair. It was a big birthday party, and we wanted to come to that, too. But we didn't. We stayed home, and I began to get sleepy about 7 o'clock.

As I was sitting on the sofa with Jackie getting ready to go upstairs, I confessed some things to her. I confessed that over this last week, I had found myself listening to Satan. Again. He's not really tried to speak to me much during this last cancer episode. But last week there were several times that he did get in my mind—and I listened to him. So, I needed to confess that both to God and to Jackie.

I told her, "He's been whispering in my ear, and I've listened to him. One of the first things he said was, 'There is no God. And even if there is, He doesn't interfere with the laws of nature. In short, Jamie, you're on your own.'"

I wonder this morning if there is anybody else who has ever heard Satan say that to you? Oh, okay. Lots of you. Well, this last week I thought I had a monopoly on that whisper.

The second thing Satan said to me was, "The Bible is not true. It's a book of myths—fairy stories. People want to believe it so much that across the years they have turned it into a sacred book."

Has anybody ever heard Satan tell you that? Not as many. Okay. I guess he only says that to intellectuals. By that I mean people who are always trying to figure things out. Satan doesn't talk that way to children or to the childlike. He doesn't talk that way to people who have great faith. He only talks that way to people who are constantly trying to analyze things, as I have been doing lately—which is why I am confessing it to you now.

The third thing Satan told me was far more personal. He said, "Why do you think you're different from anyone else in this world? God doesn't answer prayer. He just provides heaven for you if you accept Jesus. Why don't you stop struggling to stay alive and die like everyone else?"

Honestly, I still struggle with that. I struggle with it because I've watched some of my friends die who have loved God as much as I do. Some of them, I think, probably loved God more than I do. I've watched people in this church who've had far more faith than I'll ever have stand on the Word, believing, only to be struck with cancer or another debilitating disease—and then they die. Despite the prayers of the church. Despite the prayers of their family. Despite their own faith and their own prayers, they die.

As a Christian I absolutely believe my life is in God's hands.

I absolutely believe they've gone to heaven. But what do I do with the fact that they died, despite all the prayers?

So, I listened to Satan when he said, "Why do you think you're different? You're going to die just like everybody else." Now, I know I'm going to die in my time. But he was saying, "No, you're not going to die in your time. You're going to die early."

As a Christian I absolutely believe my life is in God's hands. He and He alone determines when I will die. But Satan was speaking so logically. He was so convincing. He sounded so analytical, so certain, that I couldn't help but listen.

What do you do when that kind of stuff happens? What do you do when you begin to hear that logical voice speaking to you at your time of greatest need?

What I did was forget what sounded logical and go back to the divine Word of God. What I ended up saying back to Satan, as I was lying in my bed that night, was, "Forget it. I am not going to listen to your deceptions anymore. I am not going to die tonight."

I think I felt like Job must have felt when his wife went to him while he's sitting on a pile of ashes. Job has boils all over his body and worms crawling in and out of his sores. He's scraping his boils with a piece of broken pottery in abject misery. His children have died, and all his fortune is gone. And finally, to top it all off, his wife comes up to him and says, "Curse God and die, Job."

You know, sometimes it might just be a lot easier to do that. You don't actually have to curse God. But "just turn over and die" sounds like such a simple solution.

However, I decided not to do that. I decided not to die that night.

After confessing all this to my wife, I went up to my bedroom again and laid on my bed. There, under the cool sheets, I went back to my Ebenezer—my memorial stone—and I began to remember all the good things about our Lord Jesus. Lying there in my bed, I began to give thanks out loud and praise Him with my voice.

Praise really does need to be vocalized. So, I just laid there on my bed, praising Him and thanking Him. I thanked Him for His promises, and I thanked Him for who He is. And in the process, I quickly realized that the questions I had been asking—the questions Satan was asking me—are not legitimate questions. They are not legitimate, because they will never be answered to our satisfaction this side of glory.

I don't know why some people get sick and die and others get sick and are healed. There's no answer for that. So, don't come ask me that question. In fact, don't ask yourself that question either. Don't read books that say they have answers to that question. There is no answer to that question. Why? Because it's not a legitimate question. It's an illegitimate question, because all asking it will do is confuse you and drive you into despair.

I don't know why good people who love Jesus stay poor all their lives, and others, wicked people, make huge amounts of money only to waste it on themselves. I don't understand. There's enough wealth in the United States in the hands of the wicked to convert the entire world to Jesus Christ. We could do it in 30 days if that money was released to the cause of bringing people to Jesus. I don't understand why that doesn't happen.

Did you know that these are some of the same questions David asks in Psalm 73? David wonders why the wicked prosper and the good struggle and are in pain and despair.
It's a terribly depressing psalm until you get about two-thirds of the way through. Then David says he found his answer when he went into the house of the Lord. He's not talking about getting up on Sunday morning and going to

church. He's talking about coming into the very presence of God Almighty.

Why do the wicked prosper and the good suffer? Why do some people live and others die? Why do some people recover from their sickness and others don't? All these questions have but one response. The answer is found in the presence of God.

The answer is found in the presence of God.

You will not get an intellectual or academic answer from God. What you get is His presence. And suddenly, in His presence, all those crazy questions don't matter anymore. You don't give a flip about the unresolvable questions. You put them aside when you are in His presence, because suddenly you know that you are in the presence of something so much bigger than you are, so much grander than you or your questions are.

Being in God's presence is so far beyond all human understanding and comprehension that we can only, just barely, get a tiny taste of it here on Earth. There is so much more we don't understand that we forget about all the foolish questions and say, "I just want to be in Your presence, Lord. That's all."

That's what I did last night. Laying on my bed, giving thanks, I came into His presence, and suddenly hope was back. I mean Hope with a capital H. And I realized He is alive. His word is true. He does answer prayer.

Then Satan whispers, "What about those who . . . ?"

I will not hear that question, I said. I will walk in the knowledge that I have of who He is, of who my Lord is.

So, now that I have gotten beyond the need for God to answer senseless questions, what is my part? My part is to persevere. My part is to not give up. My part is to not quit but to push through.

My part is to persevere. My part is to not give up. My part is to not quit but to push through.

I can't do it in my own strength. I can only do it in His power and strength. But when I am in His presence, His strength, His power, His ability is mine as well. But I must be willing to cooperate. More than willing—I must simply cooperate, obey and abide.

Earlier this week I was reading an article in the *Jerusalem Post* written by a rabbi on the difference between the two Hebrew words for "inheritance." Specifically, he was talking about the reference in Exodus 6:8:

> And I will bring you to the land I swore with uplifted hand to give to Abraham, to Isaac and to Jacob. I will give it to you as a possession [heritage]. I am the Lord.

God's word to Moses was that the Promised Land was given to the nation of Israel as an inheritance. It was and is their heritage.

The rabbi said there are two different words in the Hebrew language for "inheritance." One is the word *yerusha.* The other is the word *morasha,* which is only used one time in the Bible—in this verse. They both mean "heritage" or "inheritance."

This rabbi went on to say that there is a vast difference between those two words, even though they're both translated to mean an inheritance. A *yerusha* is something that you don't have to work for. It's simply something you inherit. Maybe your father was smart enough 45 years ago to buy several thousand shares of IBM stock. Now you—his heir—own it. You inherited what he bought. As a result, you can do anything you want with it. You can cash it in and buy houses for all your children. You can quit your job. You can travel the world. You can do whatever you want. And the only thing you did to deserve this inheritance was to make sure that you were born after your father.

In contrast, *morasha,* also translated "inheritance," is only used once in the Hebrew Scriptures, and that's in Exodus 6:8. *Morasha* is also something that is rightfully yours, but it is something you must work for in order to attain it and to keep it. It's yours. It's been given to you. But you must work for it with all of your strength and all of your courage and all of your might in order to keep it.

When God told the nation of Israel that He was giving them the Promised Land as their inheritance, He was not speaking of the kind of inheritance they would receive as a simple gift to do with whatever they want. He meant the kind of inheritance they would receive but would have to continue to work hard for if they were to keep it.

Their inheritance was morasha. *They had to earn it with blood and sweat and tears.*

Their inheritance was *morasha*. They had to earn it with blood and sweat and tears. And the history of the nation of Israel over the last 3,000 years is proof of what God was talking about. The Hebrew nation has had to continue to struggle to hold on to that little piece of land called Israel. They have had to fight against all the nations of the world to hold on to it because it's their *morasha*. It's their inheritance from God. But it's the kind of inheritance they've needed to work very hard to maintain and keep. They have had to persevere.

Now there's another meaning to this word *morasha*, which is to give over as an inheritance to someone else. In other words, they didn't inherit the land of Israel just for themselves only—that single generation. They inherited it and they worked for it for all generations to come.

The Jews in Israel today really believe that. Even the Jews of the *Diaspora* believed it, when they were scattered all over Europe. Every time they got together at Passover or at Hanukkah, whenever the families came together, they would close by saying, "Next year in Jerusalem." They were working for it, holding on to it, keeping faith that God intended for them to inherit that land.

Now a *yerusha* is something you can do with whatever you want to. You can invest it. You can squander it. You can blow it on drugs. You can even gamble it away.

I talked to someone this last week whose children had received a wonderful trust fund from their millionaire grandfather. Two of them had blown the whole thing on drugs. Hundreds of thousands of dollars—gone. Now they have nothing. You can do that with a *yerusha.* It's that kind of inheritance.

But with a *morasha*, you can't do that. It's like a family heirloom. It's something that belonged to your great grandfather and is now yours, and it's to be passed along to your children and your grandchildren with unspoken instructions that it is to never leave the family. It is never to be divided or sold. It's not only for you, it's for those yet to come.

Salvation as we know it is *yerusha.* You don't have to work for it. You can't buy your salvation. It's given to you as an inheritance. God gave it to you. It's free. You can't work your way into a relationship with God. You can't do good things and therefore earn God's favor.

Paul in Ephesians 2:8 says,

> For it is by grace you have been saved, through faith — and this not from yourselves, it is the gift of God.

Grace is a gift, but we can throw it away if we want to.

On the other hand, *morasha* is perseverance. God intends for you to be healed. He intends for me to be healed. But He intends for us to work at it, cooperate with Him, seek His face, do everything we can to make it possible—all the while understanding that He is the one who gives us life. But if we don't work at it as He instructs, we may lose it.

Grace is a gift, but we can throw it away if we want to.

God has given us the promise of abundance. Yet, if we simply sit back with our mouths open and wait for something to fall out of heaven into it, we're going to starve to death. We've got to work, and if we can't find the job that we think we are suited for, we take another job until a better one comes along. Do anything you can to put bread on the table. That's perseverance.

Hebrews 10:36 says,

> You need to persevere so that when you have done the will of God, you will receive what he has promised.

Look at this other verse in James. Most people don't like to read the Book of James because it requires something of you:

> Consider it pure joy, my brothers, whenever you face trials of many kinds, because you know that the testing of your faith develops perseverance (James 1:2-3).

Come on. These trials come from the devil, right? How can I consider it pure joy?

Try this. Translate "trials of many kinds" into whatever your terrible situation is. Consider it pure joy when your wife walks off with another man. Consider it pure joy when your husband kicks you out of the house. Consider it pure joy when you lose your job. Consider it pure joy when your landlord says you've got three days to pay the rent or you're out. Consider it pure joy when the doctor says you have cancer. Why? Because you know that the testing of your faith develops what? *Perseverance.* There it is.

Now let me tell you what I've learned from these two passages of Scripture, the one in Hebrews and this one in James.

The first thing I've learned is this: there is usually a delay between our obedience to God's will and the fulfillment of His promise. Have you discovered that? There is a period that will pass, from the time you are obedient to God's will to the time of the fulfillment of His promise to you.

We don't like that, because we live in a society where you pull up to the drive-through window, give your order, get your bag of food, and you have it all gobbled up by the time you get out on the street. It's not only fast-delivered food, it's fast-eat food. We like to have everything *now*.

There is a war in the Middle East. You can turn on the TV and find out almost immediately what's going on. We can get the news *now*. We are no longer satisfied with reading it in the newspaper tomorrow—or, as they had to do in Jesus' day, finding out about a war four years later when somebody finally returns from the war zone. Or maybe never finding out, because nobody comes back.

There is usually a delay between our obedience to God's will and the fulfillment of His promise.

We want results *now,* and subconsciously we expect God to respond to us in the same way. We expect that when we obey God, everything is going to go perfectly—instantly. We get up in the morning and say, "Lord, today I will obey you. Today I will love you. Today I will depend upon you." Then we expect an answer to our prayer by noon.

Sometimes we think obedience to God is like rubbing a magic lamp. Rub it, and a genie pops out with an instant answer to our prayer. But God doesn't act that way. And what's more, you need to understand that God doesn't act that way, because He's got a reason for not acting that way.

The Book of James indicates that the reason God isn't always quick to honor our obedience is so He can test our faith. He wants to find out whether we're real or not. You may say, "Lord, as of today I'm going to follow you, no matter what." In reply, God may very well say, "Okay. Let's find out if that's what you really mean."

The next day you go to your office and find a pink slip on your desk. You don't even get a chance to spend the rest of the day there. "Out," your boss says. "You're finished."

Now, are you still willing to obey God and follow His commands? Did you really mean what you said the day before? Because now, you are face to face with life's realities.

The reason God isn't always quick to honor our obedience is so He can test our faith.

We expect an immediate answer from God, and we expect it to be exactly as we envision it.

"God, I'm going to start to tithe my income. I'm going to give 10 percent of everything I have to Your work. Every amount of money that comes to me, I will make a tithe on it. I'm going to consider it Yours."

As soon as we say that, we expect God to answer our financial needs immediately. We read His promise to Malachi that He will open up the windows of heaven and pour out blessings like we've never received before (Malachi 3:10). So surely, we think, once we begin to tithe, we should start receiving those blessings no later than by the end of the week.

When you think like that, you are expecting something akin to magic, rather than God's wisdom and desire for your life.

Well, three months go by and there is no blessing. Instead, things get worse. Your financial situation is worse. Your children get sick, and the hospital is screaming for its money. The bills aren't paid, and the price of groceries goes up. Then the car breaks down. After a while you say, "This isn't working."

But don't you understand? When you think like that, you are expecting something akin to magic, rather than God's wisdom and desire for your life. We expect results like it's a mathematical formula. The truth is, you don't tithe to make things work. You tithe because God said you ought to tithe. You don't give back to God what's already His so you can acquire a greater abundance of wealth or blessing. You do it because God says He wants all His people to be in submission to Him.

Of course, there are blessings that go with obedience. Don't misunderstand me. There are distinct benefits that go with your obedience to God. But you may not reap anything until December, even though you start way back in January. Why? Because God wants to work out some key spiritual things in your life. James continues,

> Perseverance must finish its work so that you may be mature and complete, not lacking anything (James 1:4).

Are you willing to obey God even though there may be extended gaps or long pauses between your obedience and the promise of His blessings? That's what He's waiting for.

The second thing I've learned from these passages is this: If I give up, if I quit, if I don't endure, if I don't push through, if I don't persevere, then I forfeit what God has promised.

I have no choice but to persevere. Why? Because this verse clearly shows the cost of quitting. If you quit, you miss the blessings that are yet to come.

I remember when my older brother Clay left Vero Beach and went to West Point. I was just entering high school at the time, and he wrote back his freshman year, his plebe year. Some of you are West Pointers or grads of other military systems, and you're familiar with the process. In the plebe year, there is something horrible called "beast barracks," which all entering cadets have to go through. It is tough— physically tough and emotionally tough.

If I give up, if I quit, if I don't endure, if I don't push through, if I don't persevere, then I forfeit what God has promised.

And there is Clay. He'd been an all-state football player and an all-state basketball player for little Vero Beach High

School. He was an honor student, respected by the entire town. Then, suddenly, he gets to West Point, and he's a nothing—a nobody. Everybody is down on him, and everybody is shouting at him. Everybody is making him keep his chin in, and everybody is making him sit at the table and eat square meals. He's out there marching in the middle of the night, in the rain and in the cold, all the while having to hold a big gun on his shoulder.

He wrote back to us and said, "Dad, I would come home in a minute. But it takes more guts to quit than it does to stay. And I'm a coward."

He stuck it out and retired five years ago as a Major General in the Army.

You see, you can and you *must* persevere, because there is a high cost to quitting.

You must persevere, because there is a high cost to quitting.

As for me, I know that if I fold my tent now and quit, then the pain I've already experienced and the suffering I've already walked through are for nothing. All the things I've learned throughout this entire ordeal will have been wasted, and the future blessings God has promised for my children and my grandchildren and many others around me will be gone. Everybody will have to start over again.

I, you—we can't afford to stop. We simply can't afford to quit. We must finish the work the Lord has given us, so we can be complete.

Let's look at one more passage of scripture before we leave: Philippians 2:12-13. This seems to be a problem passage for a lot of people. So many get hung up on it, but I don't know how to get away from it:

> "Therefore my dear friends, as you have always obeyed—not only in my presence, but now much more in my absence—continue to work out your salvation with fear and trembling . . ." (Philippians 2:12).

Perhaps a better translation is to "walk out your salvation with fear and trembling." Paul is not talking about doing good works in order to be saved. Not at all. He's saying that after you're saved, salvation is something to be worked out. You have to work at it. It's an inheritance, a *morasha*, like the Promised Land. If you don't work at it, you may lose it.

> . . . for it is God who works in you to will and to act according to his good purpose (Philippians 2:13).

Can you see the wonderful promise that's incorporated here? Even though God expects you to do your part, He knows that your part is not good enough. So, He himself comes into you, sensing your spirit of cooperation, sensing your desire to work with Him, sensing your willingness to obey Him. Once He senses that, He comes into you; and even though He may withhold the final blessing for a while, He comes into you with His own presence and gives you the power to walk that out yourself. But it's not done in your strength. It's accomplished in His strength.

"What if I can't make it?" you ask. "What if I just give up? What if I stumble? What if I fall back into sin, or lose faith, or get so weary that I can't go on?"

But it's not done in your strength.
It's accomplished in His strength.

Somebody once said fatigue makes us all cowards. I know it's awfully hard to praise God when you're in the bathroom on your knees, leaning over the toilet, throwing up after chemotherapy. It's hard to say "Praise God" when you're just struggling to catch your next breath.

So, what do you do when you get into those kinds of situations? What do you do when you find yourself in such a mess?

Well, let me give you a scripture that will bless you like no other scripture in the Bible. Look up 2 Timothy 2:13 and put a circle around it. Star it. Tear it out of your Bible and stick it on your refrigerator, and then get a new Bible:

> If we are faithless, he will remain faithful, for he cannot disown himself.

You can hang everything you have on that verse, my brothers and sisters. It's not your perseverance that's going to pull you through. It's not your hard work that's going to make it happen. It's not your desire that's going to make it come to pass. It is God's faithfulness that will bring you through.

And since He has spoken it, it will not return to Him void. He said it, and it will come to pass. You can bank your life on that, on His Word.

All you have to do is endure your situation. Persevere. And when God knows you've reached your limit, He will step forward with His faithfulness and bring you through.

For He cannot disown Himself.

The following is taken from Jamie Buckingham's book,
Where Eagles Soar.
To order this book please visit:
www.JamieBuckinghamMinistries.com

Where Eagles Soar

Chapter 1

The Breath of God

"Watch the eagle," our Israeli guide said, pointing high above the Sinai desert at the silent figure, soaring close to the mountains. "He locks his wings, picks the thermals and rides the breath of God above the storm."

I was on a research trip in the Sinai Peninsula, collecting material for a book on the wilderness experience. For seven days our small group of men had been trekking the desert sand, making our way through the awesome wadis (dried riverbeds) and climbing the rugged stone mountains in the footsteps of Moses. Now we had reached Jebel Musa, the Mountain of Moses. Struggling in the darkness, we had climbed the backside of Mount Sinai to reach the summit by dawn. Now we were on our descent, following the steep path downward toward St. Catherine's Monastery, nestled far below against the base of the huge mountain.

It was then we spotted the eagle.

A huge storm, one of those rare phenomena of the desert, had built up over the Gulf of Suez and was now moving inland. The mighty thunderheads towered around 30,000 feet. It was awesome to behold as it moved to the south of us across the triangular-shaped peninsula toward Saudi Arabia where it would doubtless dissipate.

But it was the eagle which drew the attention of our guide. We were near the summit of the 7,600-foot mountain, and the eagle was already 10,000 feet above us. And climbing.

"That's what the prophet meant when he said God's people would mount up with wings as eagles," the tough, dark-skinned Israeli said as he squatted on the pathway, waiting for the rest of the men to catch up. I squatted down beside him, Bedouin fashion, and together we watched the eagle confront the massive storm clouds.

"How high will he go?" I asked.

"Over and around the storm. Perhaps fifteen, twenty thousand feet. He is now beyond his own control. He locks his wings, here," he said — pointing at his shoulders — "and rides the wind of God."

Again he used that magnificent Hebrew word *ruach* to describe the thermals of the desert. It was the same word King David used in Psalm 51 to describe the Holy Spirit — the breath of God. "Take not thy *ruach* from me."

In the New Testament the word is softer, more gentle. There we find the Greek word *pneuma*; meaning breath or spirit. It is the same word from which we get "pneumatic." In the New Testament it is often used to describe a filling experience. So the Holy Spirit fills, much as one would blow air into a balloon. The thought is one of lifting — from within. But in the Old Testament, the Spirit of God, the *ruach*, is anything but gentle. Here it is a roaring wind, howling through the canyons and moaning over the mountains. It is the mighty winds of the storms blowing across the wilderness accompanied by flashing lightning and rumbling thunder. It is the hot air thermals rushing upward. And upon it rides the eagle, ascending to unbelievable heights, using the air currents which destroy things on the ground to carry him over the fury of the storm to safety on the other side.

I watched, fascinated, as the eagle circled and ascended until he was but a tiny dot against the onrushing storm. Then he disappeared altogether.

"He fears nothing," the guide said as we rose to greet the other men coming down the steep path. "Even though we no longer see him, he can see us. He can see for 50 miles. He will go so high he may be covered with frost — his head, his wings, everything. Then he descends on the backside of the storm and the frost melts. Who knows, if it were not for the ice, he might just keep going up, touch God and never come down."

Our guide grinned, stretched and padded off barefooted down the rocky mountain trail.

It's interesting how I keep thinking of that eagle — and the breath of God upon which he rides. I think of him when storm clouds approach. I think of him when it seems I'm being swept, beyond control, to some dizzy encounter. I think of his determination, in the face of impossible odds, to lock his wings so that nothing can deter him from his upward climb. I think of him, even now, as I start work on this book.

It has been a dozen years since I had that exhilarating experience the Bible describes as the baptism in the Holy Spirit. I wrote about that experience, and the many lessons learned from it, in my earlier book *Risky Living*. For a while I was able to stay spiritually airborne on the enthusiasm alone. "Enthusiasm," by the way, comes from two Greek words, *en theos*, meaning "in God." But if the Christian walk is mere enthusiasm, we become nothing more than spiritual grasshoppers, going up and down but never learning how to soar. I need more than being "in God"; I must have God in me. Once airborne, I need some power to keep me aloft.

It was then I discovered there was more to the Christian life than living on experiences. Being born again is an experience. Being healed is an experience. Being baptized in the Holy Spirit is an experience. But if the experience does not open the door to an ongoing process, then we soon fall to earth again — battered, flattened, and often in worse shape than when we made our upward leap.

Conversion — turning your back on a self-centered way of life and allowing Jesus Christ to take total control — is an experience. But a man needs more than conversion, he needs salvation, which is an ongoing process. Salvation, in its truest sense, is becoming who we really are. And that process is never complete — at least not here on this earth.

Healing is an experience, and I am so grateful that thousands of people are experiencing divine healing in their bodies. I am grateful the healing ministry is once again being recognized by the church as a valid experience. I am grateful that in liturgical and evangelical churches alike, men and women are discovering that one of the purposes of the redemption was not only to save us from sin but to save us from sickness. The same Jesus who healed 2,000 years ago is alive and, through His Holy Spirit, still healing bodies. But while divine healing is an experience, it is not enough. The people of God must move upward to the ongoing process of divine health. And that, like the process of salvation, demands, discipline, exercise, determination and the supernatural power of the Holy Spirit.

Thus, when we come to the ministry of the Holy Spirit — as we will in this book — we find the same concepts. The baptism in the Holy Spirit is an experience. For many of us it was an exhilarating, revolutionary experience. It opened our eyes to understand the Bible. It was the instrument which allowed us to call Jesus lord in all areas of our lives. It brought freedom from the bondage of legalism and set in motion the various charismatic gifts which had laid dormant ever since the Holy Spirit first entered at conversion. But while the baptism in the Holy Spirit is an experience, the Spirit-controlled life is an ongoing process. It consists not only of allowing the breath of God (*pneuma*) to fill and expand you to the proper size and shape, but it consists of allowing the wind of God (*ruach*) to bear you aloft — and keep you there. The *ruach* not only controls your path of fight in the face of oncoming storms, but He enables you to soar the exalted corridors of heaven and brush your wings against the face of God.

There are certain things you must do, however, before that is possible. For one, you must recognize who you are. You are an eagle, not a grasshopper. Then you must be willing to cooperate with God, to put yourself in takeoff position for God to fill — and send you soaring. To remain on your nest when the storm blows is disastrous. Your only hope is to launch out in faith against all insurmountable obstacles, lock your wings and let God do the rest. That's the reason I'm writing this book. To take you with me on some of my own flights (and some of my mountain-smashing experiences). I am writing to encourage you to soar like the eagle: be filled with the Holy Spirit and ride the wind of God.

ABOUT JAMIE BUCKINGHAM

A master storyteller and Bible teacher, Jamie Buckingham has delighted millions around the world both in person and in print.

He wrote more than 45 books, including biographies of some of this century's best known Christians, including Pat Robertson (*Shout It from the Housetops*), Corrie ten Boom (*Tramp for the Lord* and others), and Kathryn Kuhlman (*Daughter of Destiny, God Can Do it Again* and others). His other biographies include the national bestseller *Run Baby Run* (with Nicky Cruz), *From Harper Valley to the Mountaintop* (with Jeannie C. Riley), and *O Happy Day* (the Happy Goodman Family Singers). Other books by Jamie Buckingham include *Risky Living*; *Where Eagles Soar*; *A Way Through the Wilderness*; *Miracle Power*; *Coping With Criticism; Into The Glory; Bible People Like Me; The Nazarene; Parables* and *Jesus World* (a novel).

He also wrote *Power for Living*, a book sponsored by the Arthur DeMoss Foundation that was given away to millions of people worldwide and resulted in untold numbers of people coming to Christ.

Jamie was more than an author of books. He was an award-winning columnist for *Charisma Magazine* and served as Editor-in-Chief of *Ministries Today Magazine* until his death in February 1992. A popular conference speaker, he was recognized as one of America's foremost authorities on the Sinai and Israel. He wrote and produced more than 100 video teachings on location in the Holy Land.

As a distinguished Bible teacher with graduate degrees in

English Literature and Theology, Jamie was respected among liturgical, evangelical, and Pentecostal Christians. He was considered a close friend and confidant of many key Christians of the late 20th century, including Oral Roberts, Billy Graham, Catherine Marshall, Jack Hayford, Bob Mumford, Kathryn Kuhlman, Corrie ten Boom, John Sherrill, Bill Bright, John Hagee, Pat Robertson, and many others.

Most importantly, Jamie was a husband, father, grandfather, and founding pastor of the Tabernacle Church, an interdenominational congregation in Melbourne, Florida, where he served for 25 years, pastoring and discipling followers of Christ. He lived in a rural area on the east coast of Florida on a family compound with his wife, Jackie, surrounded by five married children and 14 grandchildren.

For more information on Jamie Buckingham, please visit www.JamieBuckinghamMinistries.com. Many of his books, columns, additional writings, video devotional series, and audio and video sermons can be found on this website, which is dedicated to preserving and promoting his life works.